Table of Contents

Chapter 1

An Introduction to Freshwater Tropical fish.

Hobbyists have been keeping fish in pools for thousands of years. Brightly colored or tame specimens of fish in these pools have sometimes been valued as pets rather than food.

Ancient Sumerians kept wild-caught fish in ponds, before preparing them for meals. Depictions of the sacred fish of Oxyrhynchus kept in captivity in rectangular temple pools have been found in ancient Egyptian art.

Asia has also experienced a long history of stocking rice paddies with freshwater fish suitable for eating; they also stocked various types of catfish and cyprinid. They also started with selected breeding that resulted in today's popular and completely domesticated koi and goldfish began over 2,000 years ago in Japan and China, respectively. The Chinese brought goldfish indoors during the Song Dynasty to enjoy them in large ceramic vessels.

In Medieval Europe, carp pools were a standard feature of estates and monasteries, providing an substitute to meat on feast days when meat could not be eaten for religious reasons.

Different types of Freshwater Tropical Fish

Knowing the different types of tropical fish species when setting up a new aquarium or adding fish to your existing fish tank is important for the success of your home aquarium.

Freshwater tropical fish can range from very peaceful fish to very aggressive fish and everything in between. Something else to consider are the water parameters in which each individual type of fish is the most comfortable with.

Some fish when bought are very small but quickly grows to a very large, always consider their adult size and make sure that you have the facilities to house them properly. Feeding and breeding patterns are also different for almost each species.

Below is a list of the most common types of fish listed by family group.

- BONYTONGUES – Butterflyfish
- CATFISH - Cory Cats and Plecos
- CHARACINS - Tetras, Hatchet fish and the Silver Dollar Fish
- CICHLIDS - Dwarf Cichlids and Large Cichlids
- CYPRINIDS - Barbs, Danios and Rasboras
- KILLIFISH
- LABYRINTH FISH - Gouramis and Bettas(fish that also breath air)
- LIVE-BEARERS
- LOACHES
- RAINBOWFISH
- RICEFISH
- BLUE EYES
- SHRIMP

How to setup an Aquarium

Setting up a new aquarium is easier than it looks at first glance. But there is a lot more involved than just going and buying all the latest and greatest gadgets, you can have all the money in the world, but if you are not ready for commitment and passion for this hobby it is better to just quit now. Here is a few basic pointers to get you started.

Tank Placement

- Decide where you want to put your tank; this will determine what size you buy, and whether or not you'll need a stand to go with it. 20 gallons or more will need a stand no matter what. As tempting as it is to buy a small tank they actually are harder to maintain good water quality. Larger tanks are much more stable, because of the large volume of water.

- Consider not subjecting fish to a fish bowl; they tend to suffocate the fish either by lack of oxygen or by their own waste.

Some things to keep in mind when placing your tank.

- Do not place your tank directly in front of a window or direct sunlight as this can cause severe algae outbreaks.
- It is also important to consider the weight of a fish tank considering the water, tank, stand, sump and hood. 1l of water ads up to 1kg so even smaller tanks can be quite heavy. Make sure that there is adequate structural support under the floor.
- Make sure that you have power nearby, and keep in mind how far you will have to haul water for weekly tank maintenance.
- Choose a fish tank that fits the space you have decided on. Also consider the type of fish you would like to keep; you want a tank big enough for their adult size. Consider a taller tank if you are thinking of live plants, to allow them room to grow tall, but keep in mind that appropriate lighting for many types of plants can be expensive. Also keep in mind that the deeper the tank the more lighting you will need.
- Get an aquarium stand that is designed for the dimensions and shape of your tank. If you need a custom stand consider getting a professional to build one for you. . Once again do not underestimate the weight of a complete setup. Make sure the stand is either rated for the size of your tank or that it has been custom build to be very sturdy. Do not use stands other than ones specifically designed for taking the weight of a fish tank.
- If you don't buy a complete setup, make sure the equipment you choose is rated for the size of your tank.

- Heat the tank. Make sure you buy a quality heater that can handle the volume of water in the tank. I would also suggest using two at a time always making sure that at least one of them is operational. Look for one with an adjustable thermostat, since different fish prefer different temperatures. A good rule of thumb is 3-5 watts of heat per gallon of water. Depending on the species they will thrive at 21-28°C.
- Get substrate. Choose gravel or sand for the bottom; this is essential to a healthy aquarium. River sand washed properly makes for ideal substrate. Sand is optimal for fish that like to burrow but it needs to be stirred on a regular basis to prevent dead spots that can wreak havoc on your tank.
- Look for leaks. Fill the tank with about two inches of water, and then wait for a half an hour. If there are any leaks, its better they show up now, rather than when you have filled the entire thing.
- Get a basic setup. If all is well, open your bags of gravel, and give them a good rinse under running water in a colander, the less dust in the water, the faster it'll clear when the filter is started up. This step is especially important if you're using sand instead of gravel.
- For under gravel filters, put the filter plate in, and make sure the lift tubes are fitted.
- Spread the rinsed gravel in an even layer across the surface of the filter.
- Fill the tank with water to just under the rim of the tank, usually a gap of 1" will do.
- If you've chosen an external power filter, set it up on the back of the tank in a position where the outflow will evenly distribute the water. Some tank hoods come with pre-perforated cut-outs which make it easier to position your equipment.
- Fill the reservoir of the filter with water, and plug it in! Water should smoothly circulate after a couple of minutes.
- Attach your pump airlines or power head into the appropriate lift tube now, if you've got an under gravel filter.
- Plug in the power head/pump. Water should start moving vertically in the lift tube(s).
- Install your heater on the inside of the tank. Plug in the heater and install your thermometer. Make sure that the heater is fully submerged before plugging it in

As this can cause the heater to burn out.

- Place in any plants or decorations. Plants are functional decorations. It is difficult to make a mechanical filter control a plankton bloom. Plants make it easy. For some fish, plants are compulsory. With tall tanks, place plants with the tank only half full, so you don't have to submerge your whole arm.
- Wait for an hour or two, and check that the temperature is still in the safe range, that there are no leaks, and that the water is circulating properly.
- Add the water dechlorinator, according to the instructions on the bottle (if you have not used purified drinking water)
- Cycle your tank. Run the tank for at least 2 weeks before you add any fish to the tank.
- Choose fish. Discuss what type of freshwater, tropical fish you want to have with the sales person. Inform yourself in fish forums on the internet about your favourite kind of fish. They should give you tips on who can and can't get along, and so forth. Watch out though, some salespeople might not have experience with aquariums and therefore can provide poor advice. See if there is a locally-owned fish store in the area, they tend to provide the most accurate information and high-quality fish.
- Add Fish. Start with two or three fish the first ten days, then get two or three more, wait another ten days, etc. If you put too many fish at once into a new tank, the water will not be able to adequately cycle, and will quickly turn toxic. Patience is the key for the first six to eight weeks. That said, a big mistake people make is to buy schooling fish but only get 1 or 2 of them. This is stressful and cruel for the fish. A school means that a group of 5 is the minimum. .

Things to consider when buying an Aquarium

Keeping an aquarium can be a great hobby with therapeutic advantages. It is a practice that be enjoyed by hobbyists of all ages and experience levels. Before committing to a purchase or the responsibility of caring for animals, consider the following aspects of owning and maintaining an aquarium.

Initial Costs and Fish Selection - The starting cost of keeping an aquarium may be fairly high due to all of the equipment needed to attain the proper environment. Purchases include the actual tank, filters, lights and other essentials, not to mention the fish themselves. Generally, the larger the tank the higher the cost; saltwater setups will cost more than freshwater.

A typical tropical freshwater aquarium can safely support one inch of fish per gallon of water; this is dependent on the surface area of the water - the more surface area, the more oxygen, therefore, supporting more fish. Some fish are schooling fish, which by nature prefer to be in large groups; others may like their independence and will prefer to be left alone.

Marine, or saltwater, fish are more colourful but require a lot of care and knowledge. Freshwater aquariums tend to be easier to maintain because there are fewer chemical balances to worry about.

Size and Placement - The size and type of aquarium you need may be dictated by the type of fish you want, the available area, and your budget. In some cases, bigger is better. A larger tank will allow you to add more fish later; the larger amount of water will thin out chemicals, which can be potentially dangerous to fish. No matter what the size, the location should be level, sturdy and where it is not in danger of being bumped into or knocked over.

Equipment

Lighting

The aim of putting lights over the aquarium is to try and simulate natural light.

It is important where the aquarium is positioned when you are lighting it. Ideally you want to be able to control the light completely so a dark area away from the window is best. Sunlight on the tank can cause algae blooms and also temperature fluctuations.

There are a few types of lights that are suitable - I am only going to mention fluorescent as they are generally the cheapest to get, run and maintain. Fluorescent lights are also suitable for almost all aquariums.

The type of tube you use is very important. You want to simulate natural sun light so it is best steer away from all the fancy colours available and go for a full spectrum light (not a broad spectrum). Many of the ''aquarium lights' are not ideal for plant growth as the manufacturers have concentrated on bringing out the fishes natural colours and not plant growth.

How much light

A reasonable rule of thumb is about One Watt per Litre of aquarium water. There are many varying opinions here but one needs to also remember that different plants need different conditions e.g. Anubias sp. needs less light than Echinodorus sp. to thrive.

It is very difficult to overdo the amount of lights and I feel it's a good idea to jam as many tubes under the hood as you can afford .

Light Duration

Most aquarium plants are from the tropics where there are equal day and night lengths. Many Aquarists try and copy this. I find I get better results with fewer algae when the lights are on for no more than 10 hours a day.

A timer is a big help with this. Try and time the aquariums day period when you are most likely to be there so you aren't tempted to turn on the lights at the wrong time.

Heating

There is probably nothing more important to properly maintain an aquarium and keep the water temperature in a certain amount. Freshwater fish thrive in hot water which is constant. After all they are tropical fish. Gold Fish on the other hand are cold water fish and can handle temperature fluctuations.

The water temperature is important for the health and welfare of the fish. If the temperature drops one degree for more than 24 hours, you can leave many fish more susceptible to diseases such as "Ich". If it is not fast enough, you can create irreversible damage and kill the entire fish tank and all. Therefore, it is doubly important to keep an eye on the water temperature change during the season, especially as winter approaches and temperatures drop.

There are a variety of heaters Aquarium fish market and depending on how much you're willing to spend will determine how it functional, you can be. Cheapest can save you money, but they are more likely to break or malfunction, bringing the investment you made in your fish. Many times the heater at a low price is not an accurate adjustment of the heat, making calls difficult temperature.

For most people an average temperature could do the job they seek. His temperature controls are reliable and maintain a constant temperature without having to make adjustments at any time. Please review your aquarium heater periodically to ensure proper operation, and after a year of use there is a good chance you have to be replaced.

The best way to make sure your aquarium heater functioning properly is to invest in a Digital Thermometer. This is easy to monitor the temperature, because it is always visible and accurate. You can use the type that float around inside the aquarium, but are not always so easy to read and more often than not float on the back of the filter or other obstruction, you can see what the temperature.

Once you have your heater is best to place it near a filter. This allows the hot water that is distributed around the holding tank of hot and cold spots to a minimum. A water heater is an important part of the entire ecosystem of the tank and keep water temperature at a constant level of your fish are free of disease and keep you entertained for many years.

Filtration

Filtration is probably the most important part of any aquarium, just because of the long term problems or joy that it can cause the fish, plants or water quality for the hobbyist.

There are different kinds of aquarium filtration systems each with their advantages and disadvantages. Below is a list of the most common types.

- Canister filters
- Diatom filters
- Trickle filters
- Fluidized bed filter
- Baffle filters
- Internal filters
- Airlift filters
- Undergravel filters

Canister Filters

Compared to filters that hang on the back of the aquarium, canister-style external filters offer a greater quantity of filter materials to be used along with a greater degree of flexibility with respect to filter material choice. Water enters the canister filled with the chosen filter material through an intake pipe at the bottom of the canister, passes through the material, and is pumped back to the aquarium through an electric pump on the top of the canister. Advantages of this type of filter are that they can provide a high volume of filter material without reducing the internal space in the aquarium. Disadvantages are that they are very pricy and susceptible to leaks.

Diatom Filters

These filters are only used in extreme outbreaks of single celled green algae.

These filters utilise diatomaceous earth to create an extremely fine filter down to 1 µm which removes particulate matter from the water column. UV Sterilizers can also be used very effectively for a long term solution to this problem.

Trickle Filters

These are to me the most effective ones and easy to maintain. They are cheap and easy enough for a weekend DIY project. What I also like about them is that they can be concealed Below the tank in the stand and all the ugly equipment like heaters, pumps and UV Sterilizers can be housed in there. This option leaves you with a nice clean look in the main tank. A good overflow box is needed for a trickle filter.

Fluidized Bed Filter

This is a biological filter, and I would recommend using it in conjunction with a good mechanical filter. Fluidized bed filters consist of a vertical contact column in which water is pumped upward. Sand placed in the contact column is thus suspended by the upward flush of water. The trick is to supply a sufficiently rapid water flow to suspend the sand, but not so rapid that the sand is blown out of the top of the filter all together. The sand supplies a surface on which the desired bacteria may grow. A FBF is also self-cleaning since the sand is in constant motion and so no detritus can settle on it.

Baffle Filters

Baffle filters are similar to wet and dry, trickle filters in that they are generally situated below the aquarium. This type of filter consists of a series of baffles that the water must pass through in order to reach the pump which is returning water to the aquarium. These baffles then act much like a series of canister filters and can be filled with different filter media for different purposes

Internal Filters

Aquarium internal filters are fully submersible filters that work inside your aquarium. They are great for smaller aquariums with low bio loads as they tend not to have large media chambers; in larger tanks they are useful as supplements to an external canister filter, as you can place them in "dead spots" in your tank to provide even flow through the whole aquarium and assist with the bio load.

Airlift Filters

A corner filter is a good example of an air lift filter. The corner filter works on the principle of air lift. A stream of bubbles moving up a tube also pushes water up with it. Water flows into the top, sides or bottom vents of the filter to take its place. As the water flows through the filter, it passes through filter media. These filters are very cheap and very good biological filters for smaller aquariums.

Undergravel Filters

Undergravel filters are another type of air lift filter. The undergravel filter circulates water through the gravel, where healthy bacteria grow and break down the fish waste. Promoters of undergravel filters often argue that you cannot culture these bacteria without an undergravel filter, that ammonia and nitrite levels will rise and fish will die.

Decorations

Decorations must always be both attractive and practical; they provide shelter and breeding for many fish species and should be carefully selected. Items that can provide security, breeding habitat and a resting place for your fish include plastic plants, PVC tubes, aquarium-safe driftwood and specially designed ceramic ornaments. Some fish have rather specific needs. Here are some examples:

- Black ghost knife fish. These South American freshwater fish thrive only if provided with a plastic or PVC tube within which to hide.

- Spiny eels. These Asian fish like to burrow in fine gravel or sand and feel most secure when they can do this.

- African cichlids. These fish are territorial and do best when plants, flat rocks and other structures are provided so they can seek refuge from more dominant fish. Certain species in this group require secluded areas where they can lay eggs and/or rear their young.

For freshwater aquariums, you have your choice of manufactured decorations plus organic decorations (both dead and living). Here is a list of the most common types.

Manufactured decorations

- Fake plants (plastic or silk)
- Fake rocks (plastic or ceramic)
- Fake wood (plastic or ceramic)
- Novelty items (plastic or ceramic castles, divers, etc.)

Organic dead

- Driftwood

- Real rocks
- Substrates (gravel, beach sand, river sand, coral sand, and peat are popular choices)

Organic living

- Live plants

Water Chemistry

To maintain your fish tank aquarium and enjoy your fish keeping and ensure that your fish and plants thrive it's a good idea to know something about water chemistry and how it applies to your hobby.

You should have a good water test kit to help in keeping the tank in balance which should include the following tests; pH, Chlorine and Chloramine, Hardness, Ammonia, Nitrite, Nitrate, Copper, Phosphate and Ammonia - fish produce ammonia as a waste product. It is poisonous and a build-up will harm the fish.

During the cycling of a new fish tank bacteria are encouraged to grow that convert the ammonia, first to nitrites and then to much less harmful nitrates. Ideally ammonia level should always be zero.

- Chlorine and chloramine - Chlorine is used as a tap water disinfectant and needs to be removed before adding tap water to the fish tank. Leaving a bucket of water for 2 days will allow chlorine to evaporate. Chloramine is used in some areas as a water disinfectant and cannot be removed this way. You will need to buy a water treatment chemical specially made for fish tanks to remove chloramine.
- Copper - Copper is harmful to fish and invertebrates and can be present in tap water where it can enter the water you have older pipes. It is also present in many fish medications.
- Nitrates - Nitrates are only harmful to the fish at high levels and are produced by the nitrifying bacteria from nitrites which are harmful at much lower levels. The only way

to lower the nitrate levels to below the acceptable 20ppm in your fish tank is to do regular partial water changes.

- Nitrites - are poisonous and are produced by bacteria from the ammonia excreted by fish. They are then converted to the less harmful nitrates. The nitrite levels in a well cycled fish tank should be zero.
- pH - is a measure of the acidity of the water. A neutral solution will have a pH of 7, an acid solution less than 7, a basic solution more than 7. Although different fish prefer different pH levels most fish will be fine over a wide pH range. Some fish prefer a pH as high as 8.5, some as low as 5.5. Unless you have fish with these extreme requirements there is usually no need to adjust the pH of the water.
- Phosphate - this chemical can be present in fish food, tap water or from decaying plant material. It is a fertiliser for plants and can cause an algae bloom if the levels are too high. Regular water changes should keep the phosphate at an acceptable level.

Water Conditioning

Water quality is singularly the most important aspect of aquarium management. Regularly conducted partial water changes are essential for the health and welfare of our fish and aquatic organisms. Conditioning (also called treating) aquarium water would hardly be an issue if regular water changes were not necessary. Water districts obtain water from nearby lakes, rivers and sometimes wells.

The amount of disinfectant added to public water systems depends on many factors. Even if it can't be tasted or smelled, it can still be deadly to fish and should be eliminated. I recommend checking with a locally owned pet shop or the water utility in your area to determine the degree of chloramine in your water. Knowing the parameters of your tap water will assist you in selecting the correct type of water conditioner for your aquarium.

The term "water conditioner" is generic and does not specifically mean chlorine or chloramine treatment. For example, some water conditioners, such as black water or buffering tonics, contain nothing to mitigate the effects of chloramine. Make sure to carefully read the label before purchasing.

How to add Fish

Slowly add fish to your tank. Never go out and buy a bunch of tropical fish because your tank's bio-load won't be able to handle it. Slowly adding fish gives your tanks biological filtration a chance to catch up.

Slowly acclimatize fish to your current setup or preferably a quarantine tank. When bringing home new fish, empty the bag contents (fish and water) into a clean 5-gallon bucket and then add about 1 cup of aquarium water to the 5 gallon bucket every 10 minutes. Continue to add 1 cup of aquarium water to the 5-gallon bucket every 10 minutes. After an hour or so your fish should be ready to add to the aquarium.
Make sure that any new fish you are planning to add to your tank will be compatible with the current inhabitants. You need to look at temperament, water parameters and tank size requirements. For instance, please don't put a common pleco in anything under 55 gallons.

For new tanks, be sure the fish that you add to your tank are hardy. After the tank has aged for a few months, less hardy fish can be added. A tank needs to complete the Nitrogen cycle before it can accommodate certain species of fish.

Chapter 2

Plants

Creating a planted tank helps you to understand the chemistry within the water that allows the plants to grow and flourish if presented with the right environment. There are hundreds of types of plants that comprise of different requirements, colours and sizes.

What is the right plant for my aquarium?

Decide what type of plants you want in the tank. It is usually a good idea to stick with one central theme e.g. Stem plants, Anubais, Java Ferns and crypts. These are among the major types, moss is another plant that will grow in almost all conditions; it makes a fine addition to any planted aquarium.

Most plants found in pet-stores are raised either half or completely out of the water. This can be easily seen when the plants have harder leaves and stems. Some of the plants leaves may even change shape to suit their fully aquatic life-style.

When planning to add plants to your aquarium, it is best to follow these simple yet highly effective rules:

- Choose plants suited to the aquarium set-up.
- Choose hardy plants, especially some that grow faster than others.
- Satisfy their lighting needs.
- Ensure that there is enough fertiliser, but not too much.
- Fully plant your matured aquarium before any fish are added.
- Maintain plant health.

How to let them grow?

Lighting Parameters

The aim of putting lights over the aquarium is to try and simulate natural light.

It is important where the aquarium is positioned when you are lighting it. Ideally you want to be able to control the light completely so a dark area away from the window is best. Sunlight on the tank can cause algae blooms and also temperature fluctuations.

There are a few types of lights that are suitable - I am only going to mention fluorescent as they are generally the cheapest to get, run and maintain. Fluorescent lights are also suitable for almost all aquariums.

A decent light source is needed to keep plants healthy 1-2 watts per gallon will do nicely.

The type of tube you use is very important. You want to simulate natural sun light so it is best steer away from all the fancy colours available and go for a full spectrum light (not a broad spectrum). Many of the aquarium lights are not ideal for plant growth as the manufacturers have concentrated on bringing out the fishes natural colours and not plant growth.

Water Parameters

Plants are just like your tropical fish when it comes to water parameters. Different aquarium plants require different water conditions. Be sure to find out the required water conditions for the plants you want. You need to know things like ph, hardness levels and lighting levels for each plant.

Substrate

You will need to have a good substrate in order for your plants to survive. There are clay planters you can get to place your plants in or you can even place some plants directly into the gravel. If you place your plants directly into the gravel you will need to use an iron supplement for your aquarium water since these plants won't be getting the nutrients they need from the iron fortified clay. Be careful on the type of substrate you are going to use, many substrates can actually damage the roots of the plants.

Nutrients

Fertilization of aquarium plants has been a problem from the start because of the varied and specialized habitats that the plants come from. Aquatic plants have special adaptations for the uptake of water and nutrients.

The watery environment also offers nutrients differently to normal plants.To know what nutrients to give aquatic plants it will help to understand how they absorb nutrients. Generally aquatic plants can absorb nutrients through their leaves and their root systems unlike normal terrestrial plants that absorb most of their nutrients from their roots.

Generally aquatic plants have a very thin or no cuticle on their leaves and stems as they are in no danger of drying out. This helps with absorption of nutrients as well but also makes the plants more vulnerable to damage and disease.

All plants require an uninterrupted supply of 14 nutrient elements to grow properly.

These are the Macro-nutrients:

- nitrates (N)
- phosphates (P)
- calcium (Ca)
- chloride (Cl)
- sodium (Na)
- magnesium (Mg)
- potassium (K)

- sulphates (S)

And the micro-nutrients:

- iron (Fe)
- boron (B)
- copper (Cu)
- zinc (Zn)
- molybdenum (Mo)
- manganese (Mn)

All these nutrients are needed by plants but the proportion they are given to the plants in is where aquarium plants and normal plants differ.

CO2

Carbon dioxide is a major factor affecting the growth rates and health of plants in the aquarium, many professional aquarists use large CO2 canisters which diffuse into the aquarium. This works very well but is quite expensive especially for the beginner.

A better option would be to use DIY CO2where yeast reacts with sugar in a coke bottle, slowly releasing CO2 increasing the plant growth rate dramatically. This is a very cheap method it can be a hassle, a possibly better option would be to buy a product such as a liquid that provides a different form of carbon for the plant but works in the same way.

Be careful not to overdose your aquarium, as this can cause severe algae growth on your plants and even kill your fish, 30ppm is the ideal rate to aim for. Also be sure of using proper diffusion methods.

Plant Maintenance

Plants need constant maintenance and care. They should be trimmed weekly and dead plant material should be removed from the tank as it can cause nitrogen spikes in water conditions.

Plant additives should also be a daily routine depending on type of plants and needs and the biotype.

Plant Propagation

The production or propagation of aquarium plants has come a long way in the past few years. Now that there are much larger producers of aquarium plants all over the world and it is recognized as a powerful and growing industry more work, money and time has been invested into its growth with very interesting and important developments.

Three Types of Propagation

- Vegetative propagation is when the plant is propagated by using part of the plant itself either a stem cutting or bulb or other part of the plant that a new plant is grown from. This is the most widely used method and normally the easiest and cheapest. Most of the stem plants like Nomaphilla, Limnophylla, Alternanthera, and Rotala etc. are propagated this way.
- Sexual or seed propagation is when a new plant is grown from a seed or spore that the parent plants have produced. This is the traditional means of propagation. Plants like Samolus and Cyperus species propagate easily this way.
- Micro propagation or Tissue culture is when plants are propagated in a sterile environment using just part of the plant like the meristematic region or the undifferentiated prothallus of a fern. Plants are generally grown in Clear plastic or glass containers under controlled lighting and temperature. Normally a sterile jelly

like medium is used (agar or similar) that has nutrients and sometimes antibiotics, hormones etc. to control the plants growth. Once the plants have reached a suitable size they are taken out of the container and hardened in greenhouse conditions. Most Anubias species are produced this way.

Vegetative and Sexual Propagation

The first two means of propagation are well known and most widely used in the aquarium plant trade; they are cheap and fairly successful with most plants. They do however have drawbacks. Both require stock or mother plants to collect the propagation material from whether it is seed or cuttings or other parts of the plant. This takes up allot of space which could be used for plants that will become salable. There is also the risk of diseases which can be carried from the stock plants to the salable or vice versa. The time factor like with some species like the slower growing Anubias can be a problem slowing down production.

Micro propagation or Tissue Culture

Micro propagation is being more widely used in the production of Aquarium plants and is very much a part of the ornamental plant industry where large numbers of pot plants and flowers are produced.

Micro propagation seems to be the answer to allot of propagation problems for aquarium plants. This means of propagation allows a large turnover of plants in a very short time with very little space and ensures healthy disease free plants that generally give a better looking plant once it has reached salable size. It may also help with preservation of the wild plants that are collected for propagation material.

The problems are that it is a specialist type of production and a lot of experimentation is needed. Setup costs are generally high too, making the end products or plants expensive. However it is being used by the large producers and promises to play a bigger role in the growing future of aquarium plants.

How to prevent Algae

Freshwater aquarium algae are threats to aquatic life in a fish tank. Algae are remarkable when it comes to surviving and spreading through a tank and you will have to work very hard to get rid of this problem. If unchecked the aquarium will become like a sewer system of toxic water and your fish will surely die.

You can prevent this by knowing what you are seeing when there is a problem, and knowing exactly what to do about it. Your fish will seem more irritable when the problem starts but prevention is the best way to deal with this. You help prevent algae growth in your tank to start, with a fresh water change every week. Algae cannot thrive when there is new water in the tank provided that you have done all of the other maintenance that you needed to.

In freshwater aquariums, there are quite a number of algae and they survive through the nutrients in the water. In some cases freshwater aquarium algae serve as food for aquarium inhabitants like shrimps and snails but if their growth is not controlled, they could be a threat to other aquatic life.

Commonly found in new aquarium setups are the brown algae. They also flourish in low-light aquariums where phosphate level is high while the nitrogen is low. They are slimy and soft algae that are found in the aquarium glass, in the substrate, and even in decorations. It has been observed that brown algae go away in the presence of strong lights but may still remain in shadowy areas of the tank.

In contrast, the green spot algae thrive in aquariums with strong light. They appear as green spots on aquarium plants and the tank glass. This type of freshwater aquarium algae is hard and appears if phosphate and carbon dioxide levels are low.

The hair algae and thread algae appear as strings in the water. They grow in aquarium tanks if there are excess amounts of iron. They can easily be removed by twirling a toothbrush around them. Thread algae grows on leaves of plants and normally found on leaf edges and can reach lengths of 30 cm. Hair algae usually grow at the base of plants and all over substrate and sometimes on decoration.

They have green-gray colour and grow to about 4 cm. Most aquarists welcome hair algae because fish like Angels and Barbs consume them as supplements to their food. Freshwater aquarium shrimps like the caridina japonica consume the algae in the likes of the thread algae.

A kind of algae that enhance the look of a tank is the beard algae. These types of algae form carpet like covering on pieces of stones bogwood, and slow growing plant leaves. They are formed closer to the light source. They are soft and slippery and rapidly grow to a maximum of 3 cm. Beard algae need a stable constant light source and a lack of nutrient balance in your aquarium to get the perfect conditions they like.

They are common in aquariums without plants and can be very difficult to remove manually. By putting fish in your tank that eat algae, you are instantly reducing the effect that algae can have on your tank which is a popular method of control.

Fish like the Rosy barbs, Siamese algae eaters, and Plecos would be a great help in reducing them. Before introducing them to the existing species in tank, make sure that they are compatible tank mates for the inhabitants presently in your tank. If they cannot adapt to the present aquarium setup, they have little use in controlling the beard algae.

Freshwater aquarium algae in tiny patches add colour and life to the aquatic ecosystem. Aside from serving as food for some aquatic life, they provide a sort of hiding place for fish fry. They are also good indicator that there is an imbalance in the system. They can show that there may be an excess of nutrients in the water.

Excess nutrients may indicate that there is an overfeeding of fish and that an unhealthy plant is excreting some nutrients. Harm to certain plants and your fish are often indicated by the presence of algae and is often a sign to beware of danger in your tank.

The growth of freshwater aquarium algae depends on the existing conditions inside the tank. Three ways that algae can thrive in an enclosed ecosystem within your aquarium. These necessities are water, light, and nutrients that are basic in all aquariums. Controlling these sources of life for algae is the major step in preventing them to grow and cause some damage.

Light can be controlled by placing the aquarium far from the sunlight and artificial light must not be used more than eight hours per day. The light must also not be too bright and an automatic switch with a timer should be installed.

Aquarium fish eating habits are different in every species. In controlling phosphate levels that serve as food for algae, it is more practical to feed them with less than to overfeed. If fish have eaten and there are excess foods in the water, remove them immediately.

Aside from removing floating wastes and excess foods in the water, changing part of the water will reduce the chances of phosphate and nitrate build up. Change at least 10 to 15% of the water once a week and scrape off any algae sticking on the glass at the same time. Testing the water from time to time is a good monitoring practice. You must stop algae growth and you do this by destroying the perfect conditions that support their growth in your tank.

Chapter 3

Fish

What is the right fish for my Aquarium?

Realize that if you do things correctly, this can be a long-term commitment. Some fish species can live for a very long time if cared for properly. Do some very good research, not only on the fish, but its tank mates. It's a really good idea to get as much information as possible on a fish before buying it.

Try to find out things such as:

- How big it will eventually get and whether you have a large enough aquarium.
- What are the aquarium water parameters it requires? Find out things such as temperature, pH ranges, etc.
- What types of fish foods will it eat? Will it take flake foods?
- The general temperament of the fish species.Will it get along with the fish you already have or plan to get? This is an often overlooked area that needs more attention from hobbyists.
- Is the species known as a prolific breeder? If so, do you have the equipment needed to keep them or do you have a plan for what happens when your fish has babies? Find out if your local fish store will take the young fish. If you don't have a means of placing them then you should stick with those fish that don't breed as easily in captivity.
- Is the fish easily susceptible to certain fish diseases?
- Is the fish an omnivore, you can’t put certain cichlid species with plants.

Biotypes

Aquarium Biotypes are like themes for your aquarium. The aim is to replicate natural environments as good as possible. This does not only look good, but creates the perfect shelter and conditions that the fish need, they will naturally feel much more comfortable and acceptable for breeding.
Here are a few examples;

Creek aquarium biotope

This biotope can be divided into sub-biotopes by speed of water stream. When there is a very fast stream, you will need to consider about fishes who like these conditions. In common, don't buy slow fishes when you have strong filtration. They won't feel good and will be hiding somewhere behind rocks or large plants. But not every creek has strong water stream.

Second option could be the plant factor. Aquarium plants are the best way how to improve water quality. No matter what you buy in shops, no matter what you read in many books. Many plants mean many places to hide, good natural filtration, etc.

- Aquarium biotopes with plenty of plants:
- Southern African Swamp
- South American Backwater Stream
- Southern Thailand Forest Creek
- South American Clearwater Stream
- Indian/Burmese River

There are a few fishes that like strong water flow. These fishes live mostly in Africa. The water in this habitat is highly oxygenated due to the turbulence created by the rapids.

Short list of aquarium biotopes based on creeks with strong filtration:

- African River Rapids
- Northern Australia Rainforest Creek

Lake Aquarium biotope

Lakes are very nice inspiration for aquarium. Unfortunately, it is harder to copy this biotope, because of its specific conditions. Flat rocks, shells and pebbles form key parts in creating these biotypes.

- Lake Tanganyika
- Lake Malawi
- Central American Rocky Lake

Chapter 4

Food

Feeding your fish

It's very important to understand the eating requirements of tropical fish. Not only do you need to know what they eat, but also how often and how much they need.
Do not feed more than twice per day and only put enough food into the tank to last for 2-3 minutes. The reason for this is that any uneaten fish food will simply sink to the bottom and rot, causing the water to go murky and produce more algae.

It is better to feed your tropical fish too little fish food than too much, as overfeeding can cause bloating in tropical fish. If you notice your fish swimming upside down near the surface of the water, this is a clear sign that they have eaten too much. This can correct itself, but if it happens too often it can cause the death of your tropical fish.

Like in all the other animal species, there are three groups of fish;

Carnivores

Carnivore tropical fish are meat eaters that thrive on a protein rich diet, they have a large mouth with extremely sharp teeth in order to tear apart their food which is then swallowed whole. This is possible because they have a large stomach that is big enough to hold a small fish; unlike other tropical fish they have a very short intestinal tract. They are predator fish and should be chosen carefully and not put with smaller tropical fish as they will eat them.

Herbivores

These tropical fish do not have a large stomach, as they use their intestine to break down plants and algae that they have already ground down with their flat teeth. Their main fish food diet consists of live plants and vegetable matter and they should be fed more frequent smaller amounts.

Omnivores

The majority of aquarium fish are omnivores and they will eat both meat and vegetable foods, dried, frozen or live, they are an ideal choice for any fish keepers as they are easier to look after and will eat most tropical fish food.

Types of food

The greater the variety of food you give your fish, the healthier they will be and less likely to become diseased. They can also become bored when being fed on the same fish food every day and eventually stop eating altogether.

Dried food pellets

Dried pellets are a popular choice of fish food as it comes in different sizes for large and small breeds and has most of the vitamins and nutrients your fish need. There are two types of pellets: one that contains air added to it in order for it to float on the surface, ideal for surface feeders with upturned mouths and the other pellet that sinks to the bottom when sufficiently soaked, perfect for bottom feeders like Catfish and Corydoras.

Dried food flakes

Fish flakes come in a wide variety and are ideal as they have most of the balanced nutrition your tropical fish needs, although it is not advised to give just flakes alone because all fish need some variety in their fish food diet.

Tablet food

The tablets are quite large and sink to the bottom of the tank which is ideal for any bottom feeders, but not the perfect solution for all your tropical fish in the aquarium, as some fish like to feed from the top another floating fish food should be added.

Live foods

Live fish foods are preferred by most aquarium fish, but most pet shops do not stock a large selection of live foods; therefore it is important that you find a good supplier.

- Tubifex worms

  Tubifex worms are very popular fish food and enjoyed by most aquarium fish as they are a natural source of food found in the muddy bottoms of lakes and rivers, they provide protein and are a perfect treat. These Tubifex worms should not be given fresh as they are prone to carry disease; therefore it is best to purchase them freeze-dried.
- Daphnia

  Daphnia is actually a water flea that is found in freshwater lakes and ponds; they have a hard shell which is good for roughage and easy to digest. The fresh Daphnia also carry disease, so it is advised to buy freeze-dried.
- Glassworms

  Glassworms are white mosquito larvae and have a clear glass like body which is about 1cm in length; they are a favourite treat which most fish will devour. They can be hard to see when placed in the tank, but the tropical fish have no trouble spotting them as they twitch and wriggle to catch the fish's eye. Do not put Glassworms in the tank if you have small fish like Neon's as they have been known to eat smaller fish.
- Brine shrimp

  These are small crustaceans that are very high in protein and are an excellent conditioning fish food. They are quite fast movers and tropical fish enjoy chasing them around the tank.
- Earthworms and mealworms

  Earthworms and mealworms are a favourite fish food for larger carnivorous fish although they are very greasy and can foul the water very quickly, so only put a small handful into the tank when feeding. If purchased fresh they must be soaked in a bowl of milk for a few minutes then dried thoroughly before adding to the tank.

- Spirulina

  This fish food is made up of mostly vegetable protein and is very easy for the fish to digest. It is an ideal treat for herbivores and all algae-eating fish.
- Krill

  This provides good roughage to help with digestion and because it has a natural colour enhancer it will help to keep your fish healthy and brightly coloured.
- Fresh vegetables

  Certain tropical fish can also have vegetables as well as meat in their fish food diet, but it must be given in small portions. Good choices are peas, Romaine lettuce, broccoli and cucumber. Before adding to the tank you must blanch the vegetables by boiling a pan of water. Add the vegetables for a few seconds then cool off in cold water.

Cultivating Live Foods

The introduction of the live food to your aquarium will be met with great excitement. The predatory instincts of the fish come into effect and they can be seen darting after the live food. The breeding instincts are also awakened and very evident in the cichlids, as they change to their breeding colours immediately.

Live foods such as tubifex worms, mosquito larva, daphnia and brine shrimp are tasty morsels that all fish will appreciate and their appreciation will show through enhanced colouration and healthier fish.

The simplest manner in which to obtain live food is by buying them from your local pet shop, but a more cost effective and interesting method is to cultivate the live food yourself.

Mosquito Larva

The easiest of them all is mosquito larva, and personally revenge is very sweet. As many people knows all you need is stagnant water, but to enhance their growth a food source such as lettuce, apple or any other vegetable or fruit in a stocking should be suspended into the water.

At first you will notice the egg rafts which look like small pieces of bark, floating on the water and then they hatch and the tiny larva emerge. When the larva seems to have a very big heads it is time to harvest or else you become the food and not them.

Harvesting can be done by either removing the stocking and straining the water or the larva can be caught out with a fine net. The last method has the advantage that the supply of larva is not interrupted but on the other hand it must be harvest frequently, as not all the larva are caught and hatching may occur.

Daphnia

Daphnia is a great source of colour enhancing carotenoids that enhance the natural colours of the fish. To produce a population of daphnia is trickier than mosquito larva as the daphnia is sensitive to water temperature, metals, chlorine, water temperature and oxygen levels.

The container or old aquarium in which you want to cultivate the daphnia should be half filled with appropriate water and the starting culture,like natural fertilizer. They should be introduced to their new environment in the same manner that you would fish. Daphnia are filter feeders and feed on single cell algae and other foods in the water.

Green water algae are the easiest way to feed your daphnia, and the culture can be fed either by being introduced into the green water or the green water can be added daily to the daphnia. It is important not to overfeed the daphnia, as too much algae causes a depletion of oxygen and this in turn is an unfavourable environment for daphnia and they will die.

Brine shrimp

The first thing you need is a couple of large containers something that holds about 5 – 20 litres of water. These containers must have a large surface area. A normal bucket would not be suitable you need something that is shallow and flat so that you get a big surface area. I normally use a plastic or glass container.

Fill the container with some natural seawater. If you can't use natural seawater then allow the water to stand for 24hrs. Dissolve 1.5 teaspoons of aquarium or sea salt per 500ml of water. Water temperature should be 24 – 29 Degrees Celsius (I normally just put the water in the room as it's normally spring or summer and the temperature is above 21 the brine shrimp hatch). Then sprinkle the eggs over the surface of the water there is no need to mix them into the water just leave them on the surface. Allow between 20 to 50 hours for the brine shrimp to hatch.

Once you see the tiny brine shrimp swimming around in the water, it's time to harvest them and feed them to the fry. As brine shrimp are attracted to light this little trick can be used to catch them or at least concentrate them into a small area. Take a light and shine it into the water leave it for 10 – 15 minutes and you will see a small orange ball teaming with brine shrimp. Once the brine shrimp are concentrated into this small area where the light is shining get a piece of 5mm diameter aquarium hose and siphon them into a jug.

Now all that is left to be done is to pour the water in the jug through a piece of stocking or fine material to filter the brine shrimp out of the water. I also suggest rinsing the shrimp with fresh water before feeding them to your freshwater fish. Then dip the stocking into your aquarium and shake the brine shrimp off for the fry to eat.

Feeding fry

One fry food is infusuria bought through the mail, cultured from ponds, or made at home with dry formulas you can buy. It is composed mostly of paramecium (a small animal). The old fashioned way to make infusuria is to put some hay in a bottle of water and stick it on the window sill. In a few days or a week, it will turn milky white with microorganisms. You can also just use pond water.

A great food for fry is baby brine shrimp. You can buy eggs and hatch them in salt water. Tiny fry cannot eat them until they are a few weeks old while larger fry can eat them right away. Brine Shrimp Direct also sells decapsulated brine shrimp cysts which can be fed to fry without hatching and other products including something called Pearls which is a fry food that is made to move around in the water column to mimic live food.

Other live foods of various sizes include microworms, daphnia, cyclops, euglena, and more. Try to provide other foods as well.

There are a number of prepared foods on the market foregglaying and live born fish. A number of people have come up with homemade foods too, often including strained egg yolk. Judging the amount to feed is extremely difficult to learn and takes trial and error. It is very easy to either starve the fry or kill them with excess food. Once the fry are large enough that you can see their mouths working, you can provide small pieces of the same things that their parents eat.

As the fry grow, feed them more, vacuum the tank more, and provide larger tanks as needed. Once the fry are large enough to live with their parents and eat their food, they are ready to be considered fish.

Feeding Schedules

Of all the mistakes that you think you can make with this hobby, you would think that feeding tropical fish would be one of the things you get right.

In reality there are many mistakes you can make when it comes to feeding tropical fish, and some of these mistakes really aren't that serious whereas others can actually affect the health and well-being of your fish overall. Let's take a look at some of these mistakes and then also talk about the right things you should do when feeding tropical fish.

The most common mistake that many pet owners make when it comes to feeding tropical fish is feeding them too much. Usually they see their fish swim up to the top of the tank when it's feeding time and assume that the little guys are hungry; they may then interpret this to mean that they should be feeding them more often so they won't need to go hungry like that.

In reality when you're feeding tropical fish on a regular schedule they will just get accustomed to this schedule and will head for the top of the tank when it's time for food, whether they're hungry or not. Don't let the behaviour of the fish influence your schedule when it comes to feeding tropical fish; usually twice per day is enough and in some cases even more than enough, as in their natural habitat it's not unusual for them to actually miss a day or even two of food and be perfectly fine.

It's also good when feeding tropical fish to occasionally give them a special treat. Fish love live feed and things like blood worms or brine shrimp are considered delicacies to them. You never want to have these special treats to act as their main food but an occasional treat can make your fish feel happy and calm, the same way it does for humans.

You don't need to actually touch live bait when feeding tropical fish these special treats as most are available frozen or freeze dried, making them last longer and more convenient for you. If you have fish that you're trying to breed, you can give them a special treat as well since this can make them more calm and ready to mate.

Chapter 5

Tank Maintenance

Aquarium Maintenance Plan

It's easier to prevent disease, than it is to cure sick fish. This page contains a list of tasks and a preventative maintenance schedule for doing these tasks that will prevent stress and disease.

Daily Maintenance

- Check all your fish for Signs of Stress and Disease. The earlier you spot a sick fish and begin to give that fish special care, the sooner it will recover, and the less likely that disease will spread to other fish.
- Is the water cloudy or foamy? Does the water have an unusual odor? If so take immediate action. Click here for more about how to fix cloudy, foamy, or smelly water.
- Check the thermometer to be sure the temperature of the water is in the correct temperature range for your fish. Click here for more about thermometers, heaters, and the correct temperature range.
- If your fish's home has a filter, check it to be sure that it is clean and the water is flowing at the usual rate. Click here for more information about aquarium filters.
- Feed your fish at least twice a day. Don't feed them more than they will eat. Remove all uneaten bits of food after 10 minutes. Be sure all the fish are eating. Loss of Appetite is a Sign of Stress and Disease. If any of your fish do not eat, look at them closely for other Signs of Stress and Disease

Weekly Maintenance

- Change 20% of the water twice a week in your fish's home. This is one of the most important ways to care for your fish, keep them strong and vigorous, and prevent them from becoming sick. Click here for more about changing water.
- Wash your Gravel. When you change 20% of the water in your fish's home, you should wash your gravel, if your fish's home has gravel. Click here for more about gravel washing.

Monthly Maintenance

- Clean your aquarium thoroughly.

Chapter 6

Diseases

Buying Healthy Fish

Physical checks for a new fish

- Look at the fish's eyes

  Healthy fish have bright, clear eyes and an active look about them. You may think this is a ridiculous thing to say about a fish, but with time you'll agree. In particular, avoid fish with cloudy eyes.

- Check its body for lumps or white spots

  White spot disease is one of the easiest diseases to see on tropical freshwater fish. Look out for pin-sized white spots raised away from the body of the fish. Don't buy any fish from that tank (or any other tanks it's connected to – ask somebody at the store).

- Look for complete fins and tail

  Damaged fins might be a sign of disease, or they could be a symptom of in-fighting between the fish in the same tank. Fish are often packed in large numbers into shop tanks, so a bit of scrapping and minor damage is always going to occur. But as a newbie its safer to avoid any damaged fish, especially as you might be looking at fin rot and not realise it.

- Avoid fish with missing scales

  Same as torn fins, really. A few missing scales aren't fatal, but it's better to avoid damaged fish to be sure you're not buying a fish with built-in problems, or worse looking at a disease. Fish with huge bite marks should be avoided completely!

Fish behaviour and tank checks

- Active fish should be active, docile fish docile

  This is hard for newcomers, who don't know fish behaviour yet. Basically, fast-moving or active fish such as barbs, danios, and platies should be busily moving about the tank – a Zebra danio lurking around the surface of the water is almost certainly sick. On the other hand, a Corydorus catfish will often sit motionless on the substrate, while dwarf cichlids typically move with a start-stop motion. Until you get more experience, the best bet is to compare your potential purchase's behaviour with other similar fish in nearby tanks.

- Look out for loners

  On a similar note, most freshwater community fish should be out and about, taking an interest in the tank. Any fish lurking on its own should be viewed with suspicion; even non-shoaling species should usually look like they're aware of the tank and its inhabitants. This is only a general principle – there are many common tropical fish that will lurk under a piece of wood all day, or hide in the weeds – but when it comes to more common fish it's a good rule-of-thumb.

- Ask to see it feeding

  Very few freshwater tropical fish that are suitable for beginners will respond when a few flakes or a chunk of frozen food is placed in the aquarium. Not eating is definitely a bad sign, so ask to see your fish being fed whatever it's been eating since arriving at the store. Avoid fish that don't eat.

Preventing Diseases

Fungal Infections

- Symptoms: White or cotton-like substance concentrated mainly on scrapes, surface injuries, fins or mouth.

- Treatment: Treatment of fungal infections is relatively easy. There are a great many commercially available products for this, including MarOxy by Mardel Laboratories and Super Sulfo and Would Control by Aquatronics.

- Information: This is a very common disorder which infects all kinds of tropical fish. It is intensified greatly with fish having damaged fins or cuts and scrapes. It is also much more likely in poor water conditions in which there are unacceptable levels of ammonia or nitrites. Fungal infections are also a sign of bullying by other fish. Fin nippers will damage the fins of other fish making them more susceptible to fungal infections and external bacterial infections such as fin and tail rot.

Pop-Eye

- Symptoms/Description: One or both eyes protrude from the head in an unusual fashion.

- Treatment: It may be necessary to isolate the infected fish and treat it with a broad spectrum antibiotic (preferably by injection). A copper sulphate bath at 0.15-0.30 mg/l is usually effective as well. However these treatments will only be effective if the symptoms are related to a bacterial infection. Since this disease is usually characterized by low infectivity, it may be best to leave the affected fish in the main aquarium and provide it with good food and optimal conditions. If the disease appears to spread to previously unaffected stock, remove the infected individuals to a hospital aquarium. It is possible that the protruding eye can fall out. In this case, add a general antibacterial remedy to the water to avoid secondary infections. Leave the fish, as the wound will heal and the fish can continue to live normally after a month – the fish may even spawn.

- Information: Could be a bacterial infection or a parasite infestation. Prevalent in aquariums with poor water quality and fish with internal (metabolic) disorders.

Hole in the head

- Symptoms/Description: Hexamita spp. often exists as a low level infection of the intestines, resulting in a hollow-bellied appearance with pale, stringy faeces. Some of the weaker affected fish may die for no apparent reason. These infections are usually noticed only once the disease has migrated from the digestive tract. The external infection is first noticed as small pale lesions on the head of the fish and on the body, close to the lateral line. Externally small, white, grey or cream coloured strings trail from lesions or from enlarged pits in the head region, often resembling worms. Secondary bacterial and fungal infections usually develop if left unchecked. The condition can be terminal but is mostly unsightly and infectious if the parasites are allowed to reproduce. The onset of the disease may be due to various factors (see prevention).

- Treatment: Change 25%-33% of aquarium water for soft water (peat filtered water or water that has undergone reverse osmosis). Treat with dimetridazole (5 mg/l, continuous bath) or metronidazole (7 mg/l continuous bath). Metronidazole tablets are available in 400mg that treat 60l of water. Re-treatment is done on every third day for 9 days. Metronidazole is not absorbed through the gills, therefore in order to be effective the fish must still be eating. In non-eating fish the drug will protect the other aquarium mates and eradicate the pathogen from the water column but will not treat the fasting fish.

- Prevention: Prevent low oxygen levels and overstocking the aquarium. Keep the conditions hygienic and minimise temperature fluctuations. Ensure that the fishes are fed a varied diet, especially a diet rich in Vitamin C.

- Information:Attributed to protozoan parasites Hexamita spp. or Spironucleus spp., probably endemic in all populations of wild Discus species, and even in aquarium-bred specimens. Usually affects fish such as discus, angelfish, Oscars and Gouramis. HLLE affects Marine fishes such as Surgeonfish and Butterfly fishes.

Fish Lice

- Symptoms/Description: Fish lice are flattened, disk-shaped crustaceans measuring up to 10mm in diameter, although they can be seen by the naked eye at 3mm. It attaches to the body or appendages via twin suction organs and feeds on blood after inserting its sharp mouthparts. May be seen crawling over the fish's body or seen swimming in the vicinity of the fish. Causes intense irritation and can lead to secondary infections. Needs to feed a minimum of every fifteen days, after which it starves. Eggs are laid in thin strips on hard surfaces like aquarium glass or pond linings. One Fish Lice can easily kill a fish of 2-3g in weight

- Treatment: Treat the whole aquarium with organophosphorus insecticides such as metriphonate (0.25-0.4 mg / l, continuous bath for 7-10 days, may need repeated). A less toxic treatment can be done with a 30 minute bath with potassium permanganate at 10-20 mg/l. Schering Plough produces 'Slice'. Slice contains the active ingredient emamectin benzoate that is aimed at Argulis spp. specifically. 'Masoten' obtainable from most veterinarians is also effective against Argulis spp. as well as gill maggots (Ergasilus spp.), repeated every five days for 15 days at 1g/1000l. Do not add the powder directly to the water, measure out the quantity needed and mix in a plastic container ensuring that the powder is completely dissolved. Once the water has cleared to a pale blue, add the solution to where there is a good flow of water that can evenly disperse the medication. Ensure that the aquarium/pond temperature is between 22º and 24º as Masoten becomes more toxic at higher temperatures.

- Prevention: Do not purchase any fishes from aquariums that might be infected.

- Information: Crustacean parasite Argulis spp. Most common in warmer weather and can be introduced to your aquarium or pond via newly imported fish.

Nematode Worms

- Symptoms/Description: Low level infestations usually pass unnoticed and do little harm. Heavy infestations may cause a swollen belly, impaired swimming behaviour, damage to internal organs and rupture of the body wall. These parasites may live free in the body or encapsulated in white or off-white cysts.

- Treatment: Fortunately, these parasites very rarely become a problem to the fish keeper since there is no reliable therapy.

- Prevention: Avoid buying obviously infected or suspicious-looking fish. Do not feed live foods such as "water fleas" (the intermediate host of many of these parasites) unless they originate from a fish-free environment.

- Information: Caused by various helminthes (worm) parasites, such as cestodes (tapeworms) and nematodes (roundworms).

Fin-Rot

- Symptoms/Description: Very common disease in fishes that have been weakened by rough transport, improper handling or fighting. The fins are split, ragged or stumpy, often with a white edge to them. Cotton-wool disease appears as a common secondary infection. Untreated, it can lead to more dangerous systemic bacterial infections that can spread to other fish.

- Treatment: Early treatment is essential. Oxytetracycline, at 250mg per 25 litres of water is effective. A repeat treatment is required after every 2 days for 6 days. Use tetracycline hydrochloride at 40-100 mg/l as a five day bath, may need repeating. On day 2 change half of the water and add the medicine again at the same dose for another 2 days. Increase aeration during treatment. Caution: tetracyclines are photosensitive - turn lights off during treatment – or cover the whole aquarium with a blanket. If the fish are still eating, soak the food in a concentrated solution of the antibiotic before feeding. Nifurprinol up to 2 mg / l may need repeating as a 5-10 minute bath. Commercially available fungal remedies can also be used. Follow the instructions implicitly.

- Prevention: Incorrect water parameters, stress, poor hygiene or physical damage usually encourage the onset of the disease. Some of these pathogens can be transferred in to the aquarium by the keeper. Wash your hands with a hand-sanitizer and rinse thoroughly before putting them in the aquarium water.

- Information:Usually caused by various bacteria such as Aeromonas spp., Pseudomonas spp. and Flavobacterium spp.

Dropsy

- Symptoms: Bulging sides and stomach. Scales may be forced outward.

- Treatment: See Internal Bacterial Infections

- Information: Dropsy is not a disease. It is, however, a sign of an internal bacterial infection. It is so often a symptom of bacterial infections that it has been classified separately.

Ick

- Symptoms: Small white pimples concentrated mainly on the fins. Pimples look like granules of salt.

- Treatment: Treatment of Ich can be difficult. There are several medications and preventatives available including Super Ich by Aquatronics and Maracyn and Maracyn-Two by Mardel Laboratories.

- Information: This is the most widespread and common freshwater fish disease. The small pustules are actually sacks of tiny protazoans. In a few days, the sacks break open and the parasites fall into the aquarium gravel where they multiply in great numbers. When mature, the new protazoans attack the rest of the fish. It is this lifecycle that makes Ich so contagious. The protazoans will weaken the fish progressively by destroying the protective coating.

Gill Disease

- Symptoms/Description: Rapid gill movements, swollen gill lamellae and discoloured gill filaments with excess mucus. Fish do not eat and lie motionless in the aquarium or gasp at the water surface. Common in newly imported fish that may have been over-stocked, or in mature aquaria/ponds that are poorly maintained. Also becomes a problem when total, instead of partial water changes are carried out with unconditioned water.

- Treatment: Improving the general water conditions often eases the problem. Making a prompt 30-50% water change with conditioned water is a good initial treatment. You can also add a broad-spectrum antibacterial remedy as an extra precaution.

- Prevention: Maintain a much higher standard of aquarium system hygiene, paying particular attention to filter cleanliness and avoiding overfeeding. Always stir up the filter-bed before syphoning off old aquarium water when carrying out partial water changes. Never use non-irradiated frozen food products such as Daphnia, seafood, Tubifex, bloodworm, mosquito larvae etc. Ensure that the pet store purchases their fish foods from a reputable supplier. Above all - carry out routine prophylaxis at least once per month on all systems.

- Information: Infection with fungi (Branchiomyces spp.), bacteria, protozoans or monogenetic flukes (Dactylogyrus spp.) and / or poor water quality (high concentrations of ammonia or chlorine in the environment).

The Hospital Tank

Whenever you bring new fish home from the fish store, it's generally a good idea to keep them quarantined as you never know what sorts of diseases they might have come with. Quarantining the fish allows you to better monitor the new fish for potential health problems, prevents them from spreading disease to the fish you already have and allows you to better medicate them as you don't have to worry about the fish in your display tank (plus you are treating a smaller volume of water, which saves money). Your quarantine tank also makes an effective hospital tank for sick fish and doubles as an isolation tank should you need to remove a fish for any reason, from aggression issues to isolating livebearers giving birth.

- The Tank - The tank itself doesn't have to be anything fancy. I use a plain ten gallon tank, which run $12 or so dollars. If you have bigger fish (or are planning on buying bigger fish) then you'll need a bigger tank than this. The concept of "bigger tanks are more stable than smaller ones" applies to quarantine tanks just as much as it does to your display, so if you've got the room and the funds, go ahead and get a bigger tank. I use a plain glass canopy for mine to minimize evaporation and to prevent fish from jumping.

- The Decor - I like to keep my quarantine tank pretty bare bones. It has no substrate, which is nice because that's one less thing to worry about but also because it allows you to be sure fish are eating and to inspect their droppings for signs of internal parasites. Just to make the fish feel at home, some artificial plants are a nice touch. Since there's no substrate I use the type with the weighted base. You don't want to decorate too heavily, though, as you'll need to need the fish out and put them in their permanent homes, which is a hassle in a heavily decorated tank.

- The Accessories - I have a plain fluorescent light that's designed to mount under a counter that just sits on top of the tank. Nothing fancy at all; I think I paid about $6 for it from Wal-Mart. I do have a really nice heater for the tank (I have a Stealth heater) as controlling temperature is important (especially if you happen to get new fish that came with a free batch of ich). I have a plain glass floating thermometer to monitor the temperature. I have two nets that I keep with the quarantine tank: one for new fish from the store and one for sick fish. I have another net for healthy fish that I keep with my regular fish supplies.

- The Filter - This is the really important part of the quarantine tank. Whenever you're dealing with sick fish, having clean, healthy water is key in the healing process. For this reason, you never want to put sick fish into an uncycled tank. This leaves you with two options: either keep the tank set up permanently and keep it cycled, or else only set up the tank when it's needed and cycle it each time. I don't like to keep my tank up and running (and cycled) for two reasons. For one thing, you have to deal with having fish already in the tank that need to be moved out when the tank is in use for its intended purpose. Also, adding a batch of new fish to your quarantine tank is really going to tax your biological bacteria colonies, which could result in a mini-cycle. For this reason, I think the simplest option is to keep your quarantine tank's filter running on another tank and simply move it to the quarantine tank when you need it. This instantly cycles the tank. As for the filter itself, sponge filters are a good choice as they're very easy to move and provide good biological filtration without too much water movement. I personally use a Tetra power filter running only the sponge. In any case, you don't want your filter to have activated carbon as the carbon will remove medication from the water.

Chapter 7

Breeding

Spawning Methods

Egg Scatterers

Egg scattering species are often living in fast flowing waters in the wild. The eggs are released by the female and fertilized, and then rapidly swept away by the current. This is why egg scattering species will usually eat their own offspring if they spawn in aquariums. If you are planning to breed an egg scatterer, e.g.a Zebra Danios, you must protect the eggs from the parents. You can cover the aquarium floor with marble and keep the water shallow. The eggs will sink and since the water is shallow they will rapidly reach the bottom, where they will lay hidden among the marbles. Larger marbles will also provide hiding places for the fry when they emerge. Some breeders place a net in the aquarium, to prevent the adult fish from reaching the bottom. The mesh must be large enough for the eggs to fall through.

Egg Depositors

There are two types of egg depositors: open water spawners and secretive spawners. Open water spawners will not hide their eggs. Open water spawners typically deposit the eggs on a flat rock, on the aquarium floor or on the leaves of broad leaved aquatic plants. Some open water spawners will dig a crater in the substrate and place their eggs inside. Secretive egg depositors wants to hide their eggs, and will choose a cave, a crevice or similar as spawning site. In the aquarium they will usually appreciate turned over terracotta flowerpot. Both open water spawners and secretive spawners clean the site before they deposit their eggs, and they will usually also defend the eggs and care for them by cleaning them. Before the fry emerge, many egg depositors will move the eggs around to other pre-cleaned sites. Egg depositors are also known to guard their fry and the fry is often seen swimming around with their parents.

Mouth Brooders

The egg burying species have developed in areas subjected to seasonal draughts. During the rainy season, the eggs will be deposited deep down in the mud. The eggs will then stay buried during the draught. When a new rainy season begins, the water will trigger the hatching of the eggs and fry will emerge. The egg burying species will not guard their offspring, since the parents are usually dead long before the rainy season begins. If you want to breed egg burying species in your aquarium you must simulate a dry season and a subsequent rainy season. The adult fish can be given a container filled with peat moss to deposit their eggs inside instead of placing them in mud. The container can be removed from the water and subjected to a several month long dry season in a cupboard. Once you add water to the peat moss again, the eggs will hatch and you can start feeding the fry.

Nest Builders

The nest building group is actually a sub-category to the egg depositers. Nest builders create nests of bubbles and deposit their eggs inside. The nests are formed by the male fish by blowing saliva bubbles, and a bubble nest will often contain plant fragments. When the female has released the eggs they are carefully gathered by the male and placed inside the bubble nest. In some species, the female will gather the eggs. In some species the eggs will float up into the nest without help from the parents.

Live Bearers

Livebearing fish species give birth to free swimming fry. A lot of the commonly kept aquarium species are livebearers, such as the Guppy. The eggs are fertilized by the male while they are still inside the body of the female fish, so called internal fertilization. In livebearing species, the male's anal fin has developed into a reproductive organ. This type of modified anal fin is called a gonopodium. After the fertilization, the eggs develop into fry inside the female fish. When the fry is born, they look like miniatures of adult fish, but sometimes without the striking colours of their parents. Many species develop striking colours as they grow larger and mature. In some livebearing species the female fish can store spermatozoa (semen) from one single mating and use it to fertilize several batches in a row. This is why female livebearers sometimes give birth in aquariums where they are kept without any males.

Egg Buriers

The egg burying species have developed in areas subjected to seasonal draughts. During the rainy season, the eggs will be deposited deep down in the mud. The eggs will then stay buried during the draught. When a new rainy season begins, the water will trigger the hatching of the eggs and fry will emerge. The egg burying species will not guard their offspring, since the parents are usually dead long before the rainy season begins. If you want to breed egg burying species in your aquarium you must simulate a dry season and a subsequent rainy season. The adult fish can be given a container filled with peat moss to deposit their eggs inside instead of placing them in mud. The container can be removed from the water and subjected to a several month long dry season in a cupboard. Once you add water to the peat moss again, the eggs will hatch and you can start feeding the fry.

Choosing the Parents

Once males and females have been distinguished, a suitable pair or spawning group should be chosen. There are several important traits to seek in choosing the parent fish.

Choose fish that display good markings and colour, which should produce attractive young.

Only use mature, healthy fish for spawning because unhealthy fish, if they will spawn, may produce unhealthy or deformed young.

Be sure that the pair is compatible. Many species cannot be put together in a breeding tank and expected to get along and produce young. In fact with many cichlids, pairs form only after a group has been raised together for months if not years. In certain species, one partner will bully the other to death if there is not compatibility.

Avoid crossing different strains or colour forms because the young are often unattractive.

Make sure that the pair is both of the same species because hybrids are sterile. With some cichlids and Killifish, females of different species look similar.

Conditioning the parents

Maintaining a steady temperature and providing a healthy, varied diet are two of the most important elements in encouraging your fish to spawn. The temperature of the breeding tank should be determined by the breed of fish but, in many cases, slowly raising the temperature encourages breeding behaviour. In some species, however, the opposite is true. Corydoras catfish, for example, typically spawn after a recent rainfall has lowered the temperature in their native habitat, the Amazon River.

Offer your fish a varied diet consisting of small amounts of live, frozen, flake and pellets foods several times a day in order to condition them for breeding. After a few days you should begin to notice courtship and spawning behaviour. The male of the species will often chase the female around the tank and some fish, like betta fish, will prepare a bubble nest and collect the eggs after spawning has occurred.

Effective Breeding methods

Anything that you have placed in the aquarium traps debris. As soon as the fry come out, remove any breeding traps that have been in the aquarium before. You can also add one or a couple of apple snails into the aquarium. Apple snails are much laid back and do not attack any fish. These snails will eat debris, and will also eat any dead fry. Apple snails will not eat live fry. Apple snails also produce a good supply of infusorians and can even provide the fry's first supply of food.

Keeping a detailed log of the entire process is a very good idea. This will help you when you need to repeat the process. You should keep accounts of the species name, the detailed water chemistry, filtration and aeration methods, approximate ages of the parents, when the female was added, the date on which the fry was released/hatched, the fry's first food and the body size of the fry till it reaches about three months of age.

Sometimes, even in spite of doing just about everything to ensure success, you will find that your fish just does not breed. All conditions are as they should be, but still there is no success. In this case, it is best to use a target fish to jump-start the process. This works best in territorial fish. A target fish is a perceived threat to the territorial fish. The male fish sees the new fish as a possible encroacher in his territory and he will then pair up with the female fish to isolate the target fish. The important thing here is to ensure that your target fish is in reality not a threat to the existing fish or vice versa. For instance, when trying to breed small cichlids, using some zebra danios as target fish will not pose any threat to either fish. It should be noted that some species of fish will kill any kind of target fish, and such situations should be avoided. If this is the case, it will also suffice if you place the target fish in a different aquarium alongside the mating aquarium so that the male can see but not touch.

Sometimes, fish introduced into a new aquarium are too nervous to come out into the open. They will remain hidden for days and will refuse to settle down. Fish that are stressed in this way will never pair up and breed. In such cases, you can use a dither fish to calm the other fish. A dither fish is an easy going, harmless fish. A hyperactive and aggressive fish is definitely not the right dither fish. Calm and peaceful midwater fish makes the best dither fish. Once the nervous fish see the dither fish swimming about happily without being consumed by predators, they too will settle down and come out of their hiding places. This is just to reassure the nervous fish that nothing will harm them when they come out into the open.

Raising Fry

Tank Size

You might think that your spawning tank doesn't need to be all that big, but experience has taught me that the bigger the spawning tank is, the easier it is to keep clean. Angelfish, which receive a great deal of parental care, need a tank in which two adult angels can comfortably live with their young during the rearing process. Even fighting fish, which are usually reared alone after the 5th day or so after hatching, do well in a large tank with low water level. Go as big as you comfortably and reasonably can. My current fighter spawn is growing up in a 20 gallon long and is doing very well. The large size of the tank allows me to keep the water level low whilst also performing significant water changes.

Water Changes

I cannot stress the importance of water changes when keeping fish fry. From about day 5, I did daily 30 - 50% water changes on my fighter spawn tank, and from Week 2 I did 50% water changes twice a day. The result? At three weeks the bulk of the fighters are fully formed fish and some of them are even starting to show colour. They have the size and appearance of much older fish, because frequent water changes not only keep the water clean, they also remove growth inhibiting hormone that make the fish grow slower.

As a new breeder, you will often be warned as to how delicate fry are, and told to be careful with water changes. This flies in the face of what everyone says about the importance of water changes, and leaves a lot of new breeders scared to do decent water changes. I found personally that about 4-5 days after hatching, fry were easily able to withstand 30% water changes, and I steadily increased these over time without noticing any ill effects.

Your mileage may vary of course, but the bottom line here is that you should not be shy about keeping the water in your fry tank clean. If toxins and hormones are allowed to build up in the water, you will have stunted, sickly fry guaranteed. A filter is no guarantee that the water is clean when it comes to fish fry. I have gotten away with not running any kind of filtration in my fighter fry tanks for the first month and my fry are robust. Why? Because I keep their water religiously clean. Water changes can take up to an hour a day, of course, but I feel it is worth it.

Food

Food is incredibly important. Most breeders recommend live foods like baby brine shrimp and microworms. I followed their directions when I first started breeding and I found live foods to be an incredible pain in the rear end. Not only do you need several baby brine shrimp hatcheries going in order to ensure that the fish fry have a steady stream of food, but baby brine shrimp can also cause swim bladder disorder, resulting in belly sliding fish that have to be culled.

Microworms were just as bad, the culture was easier to tend, but I found that many of my fish developed without ventral fins, a common problem when Microworms are fed.

I now use a reputable powdered fry food that you sprinkle a pinch or so on top of the water 2 -3 times a day. In spite of the dire warnings about fry refusing to eat food that isn't live and not doing as well on dry powdered food as live food, I've found the precise opposite.

The fry I have raised in this fashion are far larger and more sturdy than previous spawns and they did not die off in large numbers from not being fed live foods, indeed, the die-off rate actually seems lower than usual. (In all spawns, a significant number of young will not make it to adulthood no matter what the breeder does. Fish spawn large numbers of young with the 'knowledge' (it's not really knowledge of course, rather a breeding strategy that has proved itself over millenia) that the bulk of fish will not make it to adulthood and will instead become prey for other fish, sometimes to the parents and other fry themselves.

www.ingramcontent.com/pod-product-compliance
Ingram Content Group UK Ltd.
Pitfield, Milton Keynes, MK11 3LW, UK
UKHW020232250726
13967UKWH00001B/322

9 781471 603341